You're missing a great game!

Life Lessons On and Off the Court

Randy Fox & Jeff Cross

You're Missing a Great Game
Life Lessons On and Off the Court

Printed in the United States of America

First Printing, 2018

Foreword

Throughout life, we will be challenged to grow, to change. Most people, without fully realizing it, shy away from change that comes from leaning into challenges. On any given day we are given countless opportunities to better ourselves.

Jesse Owens once said, "In the end, it's extra effort that separates a winner from second place. But winning takes a lot more than that, too. It starts with complete command of the fundamentals. Then it takes desire, determination, discipline, and self-sacrifice. And finally, it takes a great deal of love, fairness, and respect for your fellow man. Put all these together, and even if you don't win, how can you lose?"

Leadership comes from daily choices, momentary choices, pausing long enough to realize: this could make me better. The world is begging for people to be the best version of themselves, yet very few decide to look in the mirror and lean into the process of *becoming* that person.

You need to become that person, to find your voice, to use your talents and gifts. The world needs you to show up, to step in, to be a part of the game. You *cannot* miss this. Most people do. *Refuse* to be like most people.

I firmly believe that God places people in our path to inspire us to be better versions of ourselves, spiritually, academically, relationally, and physically. Jeff Cross is one of those people. I have known Jeff Cross my entire life, or so it seems. I have watched Jeff mentor, lead, and coach for many years and am forever grateful for that blessing.

A thread of holiness is tucked deep into the art of leadership. When you are a leader, you are calling people to a higher standard. When you are a leader, you *show* people that higher standard.

Leaders value effort, hard work, and desire above all else. The unavoidable aspect of failure is not a deterrent. We cannot experience growth if we do not experience failure.

Not everyone will buy into the standard that you set for yourself. Not everyone will believe that this lifestyle is worth it. Not everyone will choose to see the value in the game of life the way that you do. Not everyone will understand that it requires one decision every single day: to show up. Refuse to be like everyone else.

Not everyone will be lucky enough to have a Jeff Cross or a Randy Fox guide the way. The good news? You get both of them in this wonderful book. *You're Missing a Great Game* is the breath of fresh air that you didn't know you needed. The words on these pages will leave you challenged to be a better leader, aching for growth in every area of life, and desiring to be the best version of yourself for the world. Jeff and Randy remind us that our role in the game matters.

If every single person decided to live their life the way these two men do, we would have more people buying into what this world needs more of: leaders.

We need leaders who show up for this game. Leaders who show up for their employees. Leaders who show up for their teammates. Leaders who show up for their family, their friends, and even strangers.

You may never be the boss. You may never write the book. You may never see your name in the spotlight. So what you can do?

Show up.

The world needs that from you. The world wants that from you. Do not wait for them to ask for it. Do it. Be it. Become it. Leaders change the world, one decision, and one moment at a time.

- Hollie Erickson, Educator and Coach, Grace Academy

You're Missing a Great Game

Prologue

"You're missing a great game!" is a cry of displeasure fans tend to yell at officials from their seats at basketball games. Somehow they believe the screaming of insults to people in stripes will make the calls better; still puzzling.

It actually makes no sense at all.

Being wrong doesn't make us miss a great game, but not showing up *does*.

Jeff Cross and I have been friends for many years. Our relationship has grown from a similar love of the game, and has blossomed into a true friendship, a care and love for each other. He and I were both interested in sharing insights on a bigger scale from our time on and off the court as officials, but we were unsure where to start.

We had talked for over a year about each other's book idea and our lack of progress. One sunny Wednesday, I was on a four hour drive to a speaking event and it hit me. I picked up the phone and within five seconds of speaking to Jeff we both knew that collaboration would make this book a reality.

This certainly affirms that the best teams, those that enjoy the great games, those that are fulfilled with their life journey understand and begin with this foundation:

The successful never go it alone.

Basketball teams play 5 at a time, and also have bench players that participate. They have coaches, sometimes 8 or 9 of them helping out the cause. The same is true for many sports like football, soccer and lacrosse. Even golfers have coaches and caddies. Most sporting contests have multiple officials working as a crew.

Wonderful families have parents, grandparents, aunts and uncles involved. Churches don't just have a pastor preaching to themselves, there are many hands involved to make the ministry flourish. The biggest brands employ hundreds, thousands and even tens of thousands of people to meet their objectives. Even keynote speakers have mastermind groups for advice and support, or they might have marketing assistants and business managers.

The best simply do not do life alone.

They have support. They have wisdom from wise council. They understand and live out the truth that you are better together than on your own.

Missing a great game starts when we don't show up. Missing a great game happens when we try to do everything by ourselves with too much pride to realize that we need others.

Enjoying the great game of life means we show up. We play. We are open to discovering the learnings and principles that will help us along the way. We learn, we keep going, and we fall in love with life.

Thank you for being here with us. Thank you for taking the time to experience these life lessons with us. We are excited you realized that this really isn't about missing the great game at all. In actuality, it is about enjoying a great game.

And the game we are referring to is more than a game, it is your life!

Welcome to our journey.

The *fact* that a failure
occurs
means little to nothing.

What *does matter*
is what you do
after the failure.

Failure is an Option

The year was 1981, I (Jeff) was a freshman in high school, in the rural town of Clifton, IL. This small farming community was a family, even smaller than Mayberry. We had just 1,018 common folks and one sheriff, his name was Mr. Statler. Not sure if he carried just one bullet or not, but you get the idea. Small town.

In the Cross home I was the oldest child by 8 years. My mom was a single parent, and I was quickly becoming the man of the house. We were poor, but we had love. She taught me the importance of work, as I watched her scrape and sweat through holding down two jobs to provide for my sister and me. My life would know hard work and I knew that would pave my way. As such, I was always looking to make a few extra bucks to contribute.

Outside of work, I had a great love. She consumed my thoughts, my desires and my time. To say I thought about her often is an understatement. This was a passion for all time. "She" was the game of baseball.

That's right, I was a huge fan, couldn't get enough. I loved everything about it, from being outdoors, to the teamwork, to being with guys and their dads, to watching my favorite major league players on TV with my grandfather. These were amazing memories that I still treasure to this day.

One Saturday morning began the same as any other, with me flipping through the pages of the local paper. Then came a turning point. I stumbled across something that would change my life forever. There was an advertisement that said, "Looking for an umpire."

There weren't many details shared in the ad, yet I was so intrigued my body was out of the chair before I knew it. Now, this is back in the day with no cell phones or websites or apps to download, there wasn't even a number to call. The text simply read, "If you're interested, stop by the local John Deere dealership."

I dropped the paper, hopped on my ten-speed and rode down to the dealership just as fast as I could pedal.

Leaping off my bicycle, allowing it to land on its own, I rushed through the door and up to the clerk. "My name is Jeff Cross, and I want to be an umpire!" I exclaimed.

"Ever been one before?" he asked.

I proudly stated, "Nope."

"Have you ever played the game before?" he asked.

"Yep, all the time!" I responded.

That was all it took, I was hired.

A few weeks later I received my schedule and I before I knew it, I was working games.

I loved it!

I couldn't get enough.

In the Midwest, we play baseball in the spring and summer, and it rains quite often. If there had been a weather app at the time, I would have been on it, checking out the radar and praying for clear skies. On the days the weather man would call for just the slightest chance of rain, I didn't even spit on the ground for fear that Mother Nature would join in on the party.

Those summers burned a passion in me that would take me places I couldn't dream of, and they would eventually change my life.

Fast forward to my senior year. The night of our athletic banquet, my baseball coach introduced everybody and shared final thoughts, and he also noted what each student planned on doing after high school. Some were moving far, most were staying close, several went to college, and some stayed right in town. Then, there was me.

After Coach Hastings finished his nice comments about me, to my surprise, he shared with everyone that I would be going to Florida to attend professional umpire school.

"What?!"

I'm thinking, are you kidding me?

I hadn't announced that to anyone. Heck, I hadn't even announced it to myself.

The horse was out of the barn, and the seed was planted.

After a few years of working several "jobs," like pumping fuel, hard labor in the steel factory, and working security, I found myself as a sandwich artist at Subway. Not just any Subway, but the one located in Kankakee next to a Blockbuster video.

You might wonder why that is important.

There was a young woman that worked at the video store, her name was Jeanna. This was the first time in my life I felt pulled to something, really someone, more than the game of baseball.

I called her at work, asked her boss to speak to her. She declined.

I couldn't believe it. Turned down without even getting a chance to ask her out.

Yet, when you are passionate about someone, or something, the drive keeps you going. The interest keeps you excited. She was different than other girls. She was someone I believed I could really relate to.

So, I called her again, and asked her out again (through her boss, of course).

Wouldn't you know it, she said no, again!

Literally, this is when most normal people quit, right? Fail once, some get back up. Fail twice, most walk away.

When you're a teenage boy in a small town, being turned down by a girl is not something "the guys" let go easily. It can be more than a bit embarrassing to admit that you don't have game. Twice. Heck, I didn't even get to talk to her.

The strong will of Jeanna just made her more attractive.

The full court press was on.

Third ask. Again, through her boss.

Different answer.

She said YES!

To talking to me.

I was excited, and a bit nervous, to finally have my chance to ask her out. Which I did.

Believe it or not, she said YES!

Well, kind of.

Her exact words were, "If I say yes, will you stop bothering me?"

We were together from that time on, and what a ride it has been. We married just over a year later and, at the time of this publication, we'll be celebrating our 26th wedding anniversary.

Failure *is* an option!

Back to umpiring.

Just before Jeanna and I married, she was fully in and understood the passion I had for baseball and umpiring. She wanted to see me fulfilled in life, she wanted to share in the joy of my dream come true.

She was paramount in pulling me out of the rat race, the running from job to job and pushed me to go for it. Her belief in me was so strong. Her desire to help me win was vital to me, and her wisdom was just being revealed. This was a woman I needed in my life for many reasons, not to mention that she could see the opportunity for us to have an amazing life together.

I knew what to do. I had to pursue my passion.

It was January 2, 1992, when I arrived at Professional Umpire School in Florida. It was winter, and the sun was shining.

There was the diamond, and with it, the opportunity to change my life.

Along with another 120 guys, dreaming the same dream, I engulfed myself into the rigorous training. Day after day, we demonstrated through drills, classroom sessions, play calling and more that we had the goods to be in the pros.

Then the day came, the big announcement. Who would make it? Who would see their dream come true? Who would go home, devastated?

They would only keep 15 of us. That was it, just 15.

After the names had all been called, they shared my ranking with me.

I was number 16.

Defeated, devastated, and dumbfounded.

The next couple of hours were full of sobbing, self-pity, and wallowing in the wake of the news.

I was a hot mess.

Number 100 would have been better, I thought. Tell me I'm terrible and send me home.

Sixteen, ouch!

It hurt.

I'm the one on the bubble that heads home thinking about the one call, the one moment, that one smile or smirk that made the difference.

Returning to Jeanna and Illinois, I nearly decided to quit altogether. I was ready to give up and just go on living a "normal life" working a nine to five job, somewhere, anywhere, who cares. It seemed at the time accepting that fate would be much easier than getting told you weren't good enough to do what you loved.

See, this was more than being turned down for a job, they crushed my soul. The 13-year old that raced his bike to the dealership to be an umpire had fallen. The dream was gone.

Oh, I spent some time umpiring high school and small college games and eventually moved on to work Division I baseball games. It was good, don't get me wrong. More importantly, I made some great friends along the journey. There are so many good memories from those days, yet, watching some of my friends that did make it, that was hard. I was happy for them, but I was still unfulfilled.

Then, literally out of nowhere, something unexpected showed up in my life.

Some umpire friends of mine that were also basketball officials suggested I get involved in that game too. I didn't understand why.

Why would this average height, bald, white guy, who had never played basketball, didn't watch much of it, and really didn't know the game, be a good official?

Like Jeanna did to me several years prior, I said no.

And like me, they came back asking again.

I said no again.

I was able to fight off the requests and the urge to officiate basketball for nearly four years before I, like Jeanna, finally caved in and agreed to give it a try.

The early years in my basketball officiating career were full of working kid's games. Little kids. Like 4-foot tall third and fourth graders running all over the place in small gyms. Old scoreboards, bad lighting, no locker rooms, and final scores of 5 – 3.

I worked around fifteen games my first weekend. The time flew by. The experience was exhilarating. Never would I have thought something like this would happen, that baseball would become somewhat of an afterthought, and basketball would consume me. Yet, that is exactly what happened.

I was in love with it, all of it! From the fast pace of the game, to the constant communication with partners, players and coaches, to the ongoing challenge of making split second decisions. Not to mention, it was just flat out fun!

There was just one regret, I wish I had started sooner.

As the games and years went along, the opportunities came as well. What a ride this journey has been.

Fast forward nearly two decades later.

We are so blessed with two wonderful children. The game of basketball has provided for us and allowed me to be the main breadwinner as an official. Conferences like the Big 10, Missouri Valley and many others have honored me with the opportunity to work their games. I've officiated over 1500 NCAA games, including post season and conference tournament games. The best part, some of my best friends in life have come from this amazing game.

Remember the life change I mentioned? We all thought it would be from baseball. Now, looking back, that was just a season to pass through. An experience to prepare me for even more to come.

Let me be clear, none of this success, none of this incredible life journey would have been *possible without the failure.*

So many incredible gifts, opportunities, real life experiences and relationships have been enjoyed and treasured because of my affiliation with the game I love so much.

It is important to put perspective on this journey, as we remember it started with several moments of failure.

My friends, failure *is* an option.

Failure is what shaped me and my life decisions.

Failure is what brought Jeanna and I together.

Failure in baseball led to success in basketball, and, most importantly, failure is what positioned me for a great game, and enjoy an even better life. As you consider how the process of failure can shape and improve your life, check out these insights from my good friend, Randy Fox.

Failure really *is* an option, although we don't always see it that way.

Many of you may have heard from people, society, the media, your bosses, teachers, and even your family and friends that failure isn't an option. That we must always win. Sure we want to win, but always winning is not realistic. How can you have a life where you must always succeed and climb to a life of better?

The life of "er."

Faster.

Richer.

Thinner.

Stronger.

Winner.

Some people live life with these kinds of mottos: there is no try, just do, or, only the strong survive, or, success in life is all that matters. Those people are missing a key element to a great game.

This is important: living life trying not to fail is not attainable, or even enjoyable. The drive to avoid failure, to be perfect is a life that says you're *not* good enough. This type of life is not sustainable because we are *humans*, not perfect.

You may have people in your life or hear these types of messages from the world, if I may be so bold, don't listen to them!

See, in life, we fail. All of us do. Truth be told, we will fail many times.

Things don't always go as planned. Our dreams may elude us for a time. We step in the wrong direction or make a bad decision. We get turned down for the date, or the job, or the promotion.

This process of failure will reveal your soul, do not let it be the descriptor of you as a person.

These temporary moments in life where the mark is missed are the real set of scales to determine your worth.

The fact a failure occurs means little to nothing. What does matter is what you do after the failure.

As you press forward and face failure, keep these key points in mind:

1. **Choose to keep going**

    You are still here, and you matter to the world. You have work to do, so keep moving forward. Remember, failure describes an event, a happening, it never describes a human being.

    There is a choice to be made after you experience failure. You can choose to wallow in it, or work on it. You can choose to sit or keep going. The choice is yours.

    You know why the windshield in your car is so large compared to the size of your rear view mirror? It's obvious, you're moving forward nearly 99% of your driving time. You need to stay focused on what lies ahead or you will crash the car. Your life is the same.

    Stay focused and keep looking to the horizon and moving forward!

2. **Choose to learn**

    Look back on the events and learn from them. Figure out what went well and build upon those elements, while seeking an opportunity to improve. Always be improving, always find what can be learned.

    It is amazing to me to watch basketball teams throughout a season, and even players over their career. They don't win every game, no team does, forever. No player makes every basket. Players commit turnovers and they make other bad decisions. Yet, do you know what happens as November rolls into March? The players and teams that learn the most, improve the most. They practice, they adjust, they learn how to be ready for the next opportunity.

You can do the same. Keep learning and growing!

3. Choose to forgive

Forgiveness can be hard, yet it is so critical to freedom. When failure occurs, you need to forgive. And start with yourself. Forgive yourself and move on. It will be hard to do numbers one and two above if you are stuck in the muck of your shame. Move on, give yourself some grace and forgive.

Yes, you need to forgive others too. Some failures may be at the hand of other people. Whether intentional or not, you need to release yourself from the capture of the bitterness that comes when you hold a grudge. Forgive them. Give yourself permission to not allow your life to be determined solely by others.

Think of forgiveness as powerful, freeing and necessary to move on from failure.

Final thought on failure.

When you are choosing the above steps, you are doing something the elite do.

You are choosing to be *refined by failure instead of defined by it.*

What a great choice that is!

To be someone
that *enjoys* a great game,
you must realize
this most humbling reality:
it's not *about you*.

It's Not About You

Failure does something amazing, if we let it. We become refined. That refinement, those experiences, our development and improved skills, all become part of a much larger process.

We become a person prepared for life. We become a person ready to make a difference. We become a person others will learn from. We become a person that makes the game great for ourselves and for others.

We become a leader others will follow.

Missing a great game happens when we believe that the game is all about us. What we want. What we deserve. What we expect.

This couldn't be further from the truth.

Here is the truth:

To be someone that enjoys a great game, you must realize this most humbling reality, *it's not about you.*

Leadership is so critical to your success. It is so critical to your growth and the growth of those around you.

We said from the start that we don't do life alone. We need each other. We need to work with and have leaders that help us, and we need to help others with our leadership.

The way you become better is by following a great leader that will build you up. It wasn't about them, they led for you. They invested in you.

In turn, this continues as you develop the next leader. Their role is to grow to a point to then develop the next leader. And so goes this great cycle that sustains success. The cycle that helps everyone never miss a great game.

Leaders develop leaders that develop leaders that develop... you get it.

The reality is that our world is full of blind followers. We have people moving around life like cars on the highway. They just follow the person in front of them, at whatever speed is set. Like cattle to slaughter, they don't even know where or why they are going somewhere.

Now, following the right leaders is a good thing, but just blindly following whomever will get you to who knows where.

Are you the person that will lead others someplace great? Will you be the leader the world is starving for? Will you be the leader that helps others get a great game in their life?

To help you get there, let's unpack these three important aspects of leadership and how it truly isn't about you:

1. **Leaders set the foundation**

    Do you get frustrated when people aren't on time?

    How about when someone misses the project deadline?

    What happens to teams when they don't know their roles and, in turn, don't do their individual part?

    Or what about the person that wants credit for every idea, and only their ideas can work? How does that seem to work out?

    There are so many examples of what can go wrong that causes teams to lose, or people to quit, or success to be out of reach. The process to keep striving, to get better, to improve the odds for success doesn't start with a process at all.

    It starts with a person.

    The leader.

    The leader sets the foundation.

    How?

    Here are 10 ways great leaders set the foundation:
    - Show up on time, and are typically early
    - Hit their deadlines
    - Speak clearly as to everyone's role
    - Hold people accountable
    - Do more than the minimum
    - Publicly give credit to others

- Accept responsibility for themselves
- Are honest and insist on it from others, always
- Willingly show grace
- Find joy in all things

Set the tone for yourself, your team, your family, your co-workers with this list, and you are onto something special. The tone will be set.

The expectations are clear, and from your example, others will follow.

Leaders build others up for success

Many years ago I (Randy), started out on a long drive to a game. My emotions and energy was similar to a child heading to Disney, full of excitement, anticipation and pure wonder.

See, this wasn't just any other game.

This night, my crew chief, our leader, one of the partners I would get to blow the whistle with, was one of the best in the business.

She worked in the WNBA, tossed the ball in numerous NCAA playoff games, including multiple Division I national championships, and had taught me over the years in summer camps.

This was going to be something wonderful. I was so excited for the opportunity to share the court with her for the first time ever.

To be honest, I was a little nervous.

I wasn't in her league, not even in the same vicinity of her credentials or talent. I knew it would get a bit real, the pressure to perform to her standards would be high. Yet, like the young child going to Disney, I was ready to go!

I arrived first. She and our other partner walked in the locker room, and before I knew it, she embraced me with a big bear hug. "How are you Randy? So great to see you!"

As we sat down, she asked me about my wife, my children and about all the good going on in my life. I shared a few things, and she kept inquiring with real interest.

It was now time to prepare for the game. She moved the questions to all of us, our crew. Several questions about rules, situations, use of the replay monitor, etc. All questions she wanted us to answer and discuss.

The last thing she said as we walked to the floor was, "If I have a double whistle with either of you, I want you to take the foul to the table." Why does this matter? If two officials blow their whistles, only one can make a call and take it to the table.

During the game, two key plays still stick out from this day. Great learning moments for us all.

Play one: Team A was on offense and drove the ball to the basket. The coach thought his player was fouled.

I didn't call a foul. I was on the opposite side of the floor from the benches and as we ran down the floor, he yelled something in my direction. I didn't hear it completely; but our crew chief did. Before I could even turn my head, she had stopped, put up her hand and warned the coach.

Play two: Team A was on offense trying to score, and the ball became loose. As the ball was heading out of bounds, a player from Team A tried to save it with a toss back to the court. The ball was caught by Team B and Team A simultaneously, a jump ball; which is what I called. My crew chief thought Team B caught it first, so she wanted to reset the shot clock since there was a change of possession. I disagreed. We discussed, and ended up going with her call.

I realize not everyone cares or knows the rules of the game, just stay with me.

After the game, we viewed this second play on video in the locker room. I was correct, it was basically caught and possessed at the same time, so the shot clock should not have been reset. This is exactly what she said to me, "Randy, I had no business coming in on the play, I was wrong."

Just from this one game, from the moment we walked in the locker room to the moment we left 5 hours later, I experienced many of the non-negotiable elements on how great leaders build up others for success.

Check this out, she:

- Started with a warm greeting
- Had real interest and concern in me and what matters to me and my family
- Taught us by asking questions that you can create natural, unforced dialogue
- Put the spotlight on us, not herself
- Had my back in a tight spot, by addressing the coach
- Was willing to admit she was wrong

That game proved to be a stepping stone for me. Her leadership made me a better official, and a better leader.

The greatest leaders bring the best out of others.

Amazing how one moment can help change one life and the lives of others. All so they don't miss a great game.

Since then, I have incorporated many of those techniques in my leadership. You can too.

2. The tower is built on trust

If you have read Randy's book *Game Plan*, or heard one of us speak, you may be familiar with part of this next story.

Early in my (Jeff's) officiating journey, I had a night to remember, or forget.

To protect the innocent, I will change the names of the infamous crew of three to Larry, Moe, and Curly.

Larry makes a foul call on a shot attempt. Moe walks past Larry and tells her "the ball went in." Naturally, Larry is appreciative of the information and trusts her teammate, so she reports the foul and counts the basket.

The place erupts! The coach goes nuts.

Larry is shell-shocked.

In a panic she quickly runs over to Curly, trying to hide her head in the sand like an ostrich. "Curly, did you see the ball go in?"

Curly simply says, "What ball?"

Oh my, what a response! What ball? The basketball, knuckle head. Ever feel that way about a teammate, or even yourself?

Curly is beside herself and turns back to Moe, and with a bit more frustration and expectation, "Moe, are you sure that ball went in?"

"Not anymore!" claims Moe.

So, our crew isn't sure what to do.

Larry now heads over to the scorers table, where the woman keeping the score book has glasses on so thick she can see the future!

The young man next to her running the clock is texting his friend about what they will be doing tonight after the game.

Wow!

Tough spot, huh?!

In the end, we counted the basket.

Of course, the game goes into overtime and the team we awarded those 2 unearned points to wins the game.

And they shouldn't have.

Upon review of the film the next morning, and the uncomfortable call from our conference coordinator, we learned the ball did NOT go in.

Not only was an error made, but our inaccurate ruling changed the outcome of the game. Ouch!

You've been there, and you may be there again.

We all have these moments.

For the record, I'm Moe in the story here. I started this whole mess of thinking the ball went in when it actually didn't.

I was sick, just sick, and very worried about my officiating future. Yet, I didn't have much time to think about it, I had to work another game just a few days later.

I thought about "skipping" this next game, but in the end, realized not showing up was worse than facing the storm. I had to get back on the horse. I needed to walk back out there and be better.

During the course of this next game, a similar situation arose.

A foul occurred, and my officiating partner, Sam, was walking to the table to report the foul.

I'm watching him and realize he didn't see the ball go in. All I could think was, "Oh no, here we go again!"

Quickly, almost frantically, I ran over to Sam, panting like a dog, "Sam, Sam, that…that…that ball went in."

Sam is a close friend of mine. Sam knew what had happened just a few days prior. Sam knew my fears and the anxiety.

Without hesitation, Sam turns, looks me dead in the eye and asks, "Can I *trust* you?"

This might seem like a day-time drama, but both game situations are absolutely true.

Those words that Sam said, actually that one word, trust, is the main point of sharing this with you. That stopped me in my tracks.

Leaders need to be trustworthy. You need to be someone others trust, just like Larry and Sam were counting on me.

Whether the moments are small or big, the influence you have, the opportunity you have to be a leader and a person others trust, is always present.

Without trust, you have nothing.
With trust, you have everything.

Let's go back to the phone call with my conference coordinator.

After she informed me about the ball not going in, I experienced a life changing leadership moment.

She affirmed that we did the right things by asking the table. She was pleased with my honesty in owning my judgment on the court, and for accepting responsibility for the incorrect outcome. She asked me what I learned from this. She encouraged me to move forward.

In short, she built me up for success, set the tone for the future, and confirmed her trust in me. All of this increased my trust in her.

See, leaders realize it isn't about themselves. Great leaders are trustworthy in all things because their motives are pure for the success of others.

The pillar is built on trust. The focus of the growth of that pillar is others.

Will you choose to be the leader the world is waiting for?

It's about
your attitude.

Win or lose.

You *choose.*

The Inner Game

Playing a game involves multiple aspects.

There are rules, opponents and obstacles, as well as strategy, skill, teamwork, practice, performing under pressure and much more. Each of these are common elements in games.

Just knowing what these aspects are is one thing. Winning those games takes excellence and a mastery in all those different aspects.

Through decades of being inside thousands of games, watching teams win and lose every night and with our good fortune to be a part of so many different officiating crews, there is one aspect of games that drives most of the successes and failures. This might even be something you haven't given much thought to.

It all starts with the six inches between your ears.

Your *inner game.*

If you have never heard of the phrase "the inner game," you aren't alone. This concept was something I was totally unaware of until a few years ago when Jeff said the term in one of our conversations.

He shared with me, "Randy, if you want to be better, if anyone wants to be better, you need to work on your inner game."

Puzzled, not quite sure how to even respond, I questioned, "What the heck is the inner game? I've never heard of it."

His explanation is the foundation for this chapter. I'll summarize it for you like this:

> *The inner game is the most important part of any game.*
> *It is the part of the game that protects the mind, fuels desire,*
> *controls behavior, guards the mouth, enhances actions for*
> *outcomes, and ultimately the source of every successful person.*
> *In short, the inner game is all about what you think;*
> *it is the mental aspect of your game.*

With that wisdom, and understanding that everything else we produce starts in our mind and our thoughts from our inner game, we need to dive into the practical steps to build, manage and utilize our inner game.

Before we go further about the inner game, let's look at its counterpart and clarify the outer game.

The outer game is what people *see*. Here are some examples of your outer game:

- Clothes are cleaned and pressed
- You're in good physical condition
- You have good physical skills for your job (e.g. running as an official, great typing skills in the office, programming skills for a developer, building skills for a carpenter, excellent verbal communication abilities for a speaker, etc.)
- Your actions are your outer game

These outer game elements are all of the tangibles. They are measurable. They are, in truth, what most people, teams and organizations focus on.

If that is all you focus on, however, the outcomes and results can be limited.

We want you to soar. We want your game to be at the highest level possible. To do that, you need to build up and focus on your inner game.

In contrast to those outer skills that you see, the inner game, is what you *think*. It is your thoughts, the little voice in your head that says so much more than your mouth ever does.

Here are a few examples of your inner game:

- Your thoughts before and after you respond to someone
- Your process when answering tough questions
- Your mental approach to discussing important issues

- Your response to failure

- Your attitude and mood swings, through good and bad moments

- Your outlook. Is the glass half full, half empty, or overflowing

Your inner game is 100% based on how you *choose* to control your thoughts.

The direction and level of success in your life is fueled, sustained, and based on your inner game. Your inner game drives your outer game.

This whole concept of the inner game may be new to you, so let's break it down with some practical application. Run these scenarios past your inner voice:

- What is your mental response when the boss asks you to stay longer?

- How does your emotional state change when someone you are waiting for is running 15 minutes late?

- What do you think and say when you wake up excited for a big outdoor event to find rain pouring down?

- How does your mood change when someone has taken your seat on a plane or at a ballgame?

- You go out for a special evening, fine dining, a real treat. You order the expensive meal and as they place all the meals on the table, you realize they brought you the wrong dish. They tell you it will be twenty minutes for the corrected one to come. What do you think in a moment like this?

- You have a big presentation to deliver at work on Tuesday, but you forgot about it and rushed to put something together. Things didn't go well, you let the team down. How do you respond? Do you pout, do you blame others, do you continue to think of the worst? Or, do you learn from the moment, realize the mistake and get better?

- A group of people were just released from their jobs, unfortunate, yet necessary layoffs. The good news, you get to keep your job. Do your thoughts paralyze you with fear? Are you worried if the same will happen to you?

A key personal question for you: *Do you have enough inner game strength to drive your outer game?*

If this is an area of struggle for you, you are not alone. Most people just aren't natural at having a great inner game. This is the hardest of the hard. It takes discipline and an intentional focus to improve.

Like anything else in life, the best thing to do if you want to be better at something, you need to practice. You need to take steps to be better, and in this case, steps to control your thoughts and not allow negativity and fear to control you.

Here are several tools to improve your inner game:

1. **Read**

    Don't just read anything; read articles and books on communication, on a good attitude and on positive thinking. Read about people in life that have established themselves in their field, find out how they think and approach each day.

    Read, read and read some more!

2. **Watch videos**

    Similar to reading, find the right videos. Watch podcasts, sign up to follow people with great content who focus on improving this part of your game. Make sure that insights from thought leaders are filling up your mind.

3. **Live life close to and learn from others**

    Observe others with and without great thought processes; you can learn from both. Surround yourself with people who build you up and bring out your best attributes. Let these people act like mentors and fuel your mind with positive thinking.

    Oh, and steer clear of negative people, you can observe them from afar!

4. **Be mindful of what you put in your mind**

    What you watch on TV, the books you read, the music you listen to, the people you converse with often; all of this impacts your thoughts. You want to think in a positive way, you want to stay strong, so seek out people who do the same. The expression of "garbage in, garbage out" applies.

Put in great and get out great!

5. **Think differently, live differently**

   Literally, choose to think differently. When negative thoughts or fears creep in, tell them to go away. As we noted in number 3, you can't think positively if you are with people that are negative. Don't waste your time with people that complain, that speak negatively, that never see anything positive. Walk away. Why?

   There's no time for stinkin' thinkin'!

Negativity begets negativity. You need positive people, positive messaging, and positive input for your brain in order to have a positive inner game.

Similar to any weight loss program, any financial planning system, or anything in life, the system is only as good as your ability to use it. Practice, practice, practice. You need to work on these steps to improve your inner game.

The great part about your inner game is you choose; and you need to choose to get better. You need to choose to remain positive. You need to choose to spend time on your inner game.

This choice to practice will help you improve, but the focus to get better won't mean a thing unless you have the right perspective. Your attitude matters. Your attitude is your *choice*.

It's about your attitude. Win or lose. You choose.

If a team loses a game, they can choose to wallow in their loss or choose to become winners by getting better. There are opportunities for learning and improving. There is hope in knowing you can win the next time. There is only despair when you continue to think of losing.

The best teams, the best people don't sit in the mud, they wash it away and move on.

You truly do have a choice and are in control of your attitude.

Those that master their inner game don't use words like can't or quit. They don't complain about things, especially things out of their control. They don't spend time in their mind, and worse yet, they don't verbalize things that aren't helpful to their inner game.

You want to be great at your inner game? Here are some choices you can make:

- Stay positive and see opportunity everywhere
- Smile more, inside and outside
- Believe in yourself, in others, and in hope
- Compliment yourself and others

- Accept full responsibility for your actions and words
- Get better, daily
- Take steps to practice your inner game
- Find something positive in every situation
- Do more, learn more, and always strive for more
- Work on your inner game

Wherever you may be with your inner game today, you can continue to be better. You do, however, need to be aware of where you are at this time and build from there.

Based on all we've covered, where do you believe you are today in your inner game?

Rate yourself using the scale below, be honest!

1	2	3	4	5	6	7	8	9	10

I HAVE NO INNER GAME   I'M ROCKING IT

We encourage you to take a step, to do something, no matter how big or small, to improve your inner game.

The world is so focused on the outer game, the skill sets, the output, the results. Be different, don't miss a great game by missing this important truth.

You have an inner game.

Now it is time to fuel it!

The mental game is the inner game; it controls your mind, your attitude and your approach.

You might be asking these questions, however: "What fuels my inner game? How do I ensure my inner game is at top performance?"

We are so glad you asked!

The six inches between your ears is the inner game fueled by something that dwells just 18 inches below that place.

Yes, that's right, your heart.

The fuel that keeps the inner game going, the source of motivation, persistence and power to believe, comes from your heart.

Deciding is a mental capacity. But believing, and truly fighting for what is right, for staying the course, for never giving up, for insisting on the positive, for striving for the best, comes from the heart.

The heart is your core.

The core of your being.

The place that reveals who you really are.

This is the deepest of all reveals; the reveal of your soul.

Are you the person that has the heart to believe that you can conquer fear? Are you the person that has the heart to go for it when everyone says to stop? Are you the person that has the heart to see the best in people, in yourself and in the world despite the negativity around you? Are you the person that has the heart of a champion that overcomes and keeps a mindset focused on the future?

The inner game drives the outer game, however the heart fuels the inner game. Do you have the heart to fuel your inner game? Do you allow your heart to drive your inner game?

Believe it. Work on it. Pay attention to it.

A better inner game might just change your outer game!

Keep your focus
on The process.
The *results*
will take care of themselves.

Focus on the results
and you will never find them.

It Takes 10 Years to Become
an Overnight Success

"You're hired!"

Two of the best words we can hear in our lifetime, right?

Most of the developed world is driven for a career, the opportunity to climb the ladder and reach some unspoken level of success. Whatever that means to them.

Take the world of officiating, where officials strive for years to get hired at the collegiate level. And that is just a starting point. The ability to get to Division II or the pinnacle, Division I, is where many have their sights set.

The two of us are no different.

We clearly remember the excitement and joy we had that infamous day years ago when we received the email that said, "you're hired." The elation of attending our first Division I meeting, being amongst the elite, believing we had finally reached a major goal was only matched by one other emotion.

The feeling of emptiness we had when the games were released a couple months later and the total count on our schedule was zero.

That's right, zero. Nothing. No games.

We were climbing the ladder, etching our place in history as one that was hired, only to find out we wouldn't see the court at that level that year.

Zero appearances. Some pinnacle.

This is no different than the person looking for the big executive job at the Fortune 500 company, only to be hired as an intern. Or the experienced teacher that waited for the news to join the best school district in the state, and is asked to be part-time, no tenure. Or it's similar to the person out of work that just wants to hear those words, and they never come.

There certainly is something positive to being selected and starting out a career. There is honor in every job for sure.

Yet, if you are like us, or the bright young basketball hopeful who doesn't want to *just* be on the team, they want to *play*. They want to live out their dream, to enjoy their passion. They want to climb.

How about you? As you look at your life, do you remember the moments of hearing great news, only to find out it wasn't so great?

How about things now, do you love your job? Or are you stuck?

How about your life, do you love your life?

If you feel stuck, this chapter is for you.

If you feel good, but strive for great, this chapter is for you.

If things are rocking out well, but you still have dreams, this chapter is for you.

The reality is, there is always another goal to reach. There is an impact to make. To do either, or both of those, there is work to do. There is a choice to make. There is a process and there are steps to take to improve as you do the work.

The road to your destination has many mountains and valleys, and reaching goals is never about the initial pursuit. It is also never about finally standing on the top of the mountain. Even though that may be all the world sees when someone "makes it," there is a story, a long journey of the climb.

That journey can take weeks, months, years or even decades to bring about the real fruit.

We see gold medalists at the Olympics, what we don't see are the years of practice. The discipline to work. The errors, the sweat, the injuries, the setbacks, and again, the work. Two, three, four years or more of work go into their craft; all for the 1, 2 or 4 minute event.

Amazing. The actual event is so fast. The medal hopeful can be on the podium or off in a matter of seconds, even tenths of seconds. One fall, one slip, or error and it's over. Regardless of where they end up, these athletes pour everything into their process. They may dream of winning gold, but they just don't sit around dreaming, or hoping, or complaining. They work.

See, the journey is a sum of the process, not the end product.

Remember this:

Keep your focus on the process and the results will take care of themselves. Focus on the results and you will never find them.

Now there are no guarantees for any of us. No basketball official is promised Division I games. No new hire is promised to be CEO. No part-time aide is promised tenure or department chair. Not all athletes get gold, heck some don't even make the team. Not everyone reaches their dream.

Yet, and really get this, there is something in common with most people that don't reach their dreams.

They don't go for it.

They don't stick to it.

They don't keep after it.

They don't work the process to improve their odds.

Even though there are no guarantees, when you look at those who are fulfilled in life, the people that make the climb, those blessed individuals that have a life they love living, they went for it. They chose to make a difference in the world.

They didn't focus on the end, instead they went to work on the process. They went to work on the positive impact they could make. They began their 10-year journey for overnight success.

Randy and I each had our own, unique, 10-year journey. A journey filled with hard work, disappointment, and growth that continues to this day. A journey that brought us each to amazing heights, different pinnacles, all amazing.

What was not different, though, was what we did to get there.

I call it *overtime*.

Overtime: a *place* where the great get separated from the good, and the *process* of putting in the extra work that provides the victory.

I was willing to put in the time to get better. From watching film late at night, to watching games on my day off. I worked to hone my craft. I spent time talking to officials about plays and rules during the long hours of driving instead of just listening to XM radio. I was willing, heck, I'm still willing, to drive countless hours to and from one site, for one game, regardless of the pay. I went to every officiating camp I could scrape up the money and time to attend.

I listened to others.

I worked to help others.

I did these things *more than* once, or twice. I did them hundreds of times, for over a decade, and I still practice the process of *overtime*!

Zero to 60 doesn't happen in 2.3 seconds. It can take 315 million seconds, or more.

It takes time.

It takes work.

It is a process.

The reflection reminds me of a time when a young, official friend of mine returned home late at night from a game. There was a play he was concerned about, and his officiating partner was concerned too. Upon coming home, exhausted, he opened up his laptop to review the play. His wife remarked, "Do you have to do that now?" His response is priceless, "My partner is doing it now, and he's officiating full time with nearly 70 games."

A dream for their family was for him to officiate full-time, and his wife was very supportive of that. She turned back to him with a smile and agreed, "Then you should do it now too."

My success, like others, didn't happen overnight. It was brought about through a set of disciplines consistently enacted. It was done from a heart of believing that putting in the work was simply the right thing to do. It was done by being a part of something bigger than me and not worrying about my final achievements.

I, of course, had dreams and goals, but the focus was never on getting into full-time officiating. The focus was on the process.

Consider this question: What will you do to improve your process in order to improve your odds of success?

What is interesting, is how people seem to be envious of the success of others. They seem to want the full Division I schedule, traveling the country, and being on TV.

In short, many people just want the *success*.

The reality, though, is that most people aren't willing to put the work into the process to get it.

We hope that you are different than most. We hope that you are ready and willing to take the 10-year journey. Maybe it won't be ten years, but a journey, nonetheless.

Your journey to a fulfilling life. A life of being unstuck.

A life of making a difference.

Here are some thoughts from Randy on building your process.

Two great words you can never forget:
discipline and consistency.

Discipline is the act of doing the right thing.

Consistency is doing the right thing as often as required.

The two together are the keys to your process, and your success. You need to consistently do the right things, regardless of how fast or far you are going. Stop worrying about winning the race, instead focus on training to be a great runner.

Here are five winning strategies for your life:

1. **Be a student**

   Did you know that a recent study proved that people that read at least seven development books per year earn 238% more? Now, this isn't about money, it is about growing. Reading improves critical thinking. It broadens knowledge and keeps our brains at an optimal level. I believe the income gap isn't because people read, it is because it represents one element in their process to be a student. Students read.

   Students also attend conferences. The best leaders in the world attend events with the other best in the world. It doesn't matter the field or background, networking is key. Learning from peers helps us improve. There are conferences all over the world, everyday, in cities big and small. As a speaker, I ask audiences all the time why they decided to come to the event. One of the top two reasons I hear most often include networking and an opportunity to learn. They want to be built up by other like-minded people, and to create and connect with friends. Top of the list, why? Because students connect.

2. Be a teacher

You may have heard someone say that the teacher learns more than the student. It surely can be true. Teachers have to know so much, and are constantly learning in order to help others. Teachers are also helpers and mentors. They help others win.

Be a mentor to someone that you can help along their journey. It is rewarding, beneficial to both parties and a way to serve someone else. Being a mentor will grow you and your journey. Your life fulfillment will increase when you see someone you have helped succeed.

Think about who has helped you. What did they do or say that meant so much to you? Now it's your turn, go be that for the next person in line.

3. Put in the time

We touched on this in the *Failure is an Option* chapter when we said to just keep going, just do the work. It will never happen if you stop or take short cuts. Hard work is hard work, and it takes time. Great things in life take time: it takes a baby 9 months to grow from conception to birth, newly planted grass seed takes weeks or months to take hold, our children are raised for many years before launching on their own, and the list goes on. You may not always be certain of the exact amount of time needed to reach your goals. The important thing to remember is to keep putting in the time!

4. **It's all about your attitude**

How do you start each day?

If you are consumed by what needs to be done, what others received and you didn't, or by what has or hasn't happened, go back to bed!

Start by adjusting your perspective. Be excited for the day! Be grateful for waking up, for the opportunity to have the day and stay focused on the positive. We can see and hear plenty of negativity in the world. We need more positive. We need to be part of the good and make it even better.

As you go through your day, enjoy the moments, be thankful for little things. Be thankful for family and friends. Be thankful for food. Seriously, start with an attitude of gratitude and you will be amazed how you can see the success you already have.

Remember, the altitude of your success is in direct proportion to the altitude of your attitude!

5. Don't compare

This is a killer for most. The constant comparison to, and of, others. You will always find someone with more, and with less. You can always find reasons to compare, you can make up excuses, or you can blame. That may seem easy, but it doesn't work.

Build off of a positive attitude, and then understand the special life you have. You are unique, so is your journey. Your life isn't about more or less than others, it is about different. Different for different purposes, for different outcomes. If everything and everyone were the same, then why try? Your goal should be setting yourself apart as different and unique by providing something the world doesn't have yet.

Don't settle for being like or beating out others. Be happy with *your* best, while being happy for others when they are at their best too. Strive to be your best and simply leave the rest.

In the end, your 10-year journey to overnight success is tied to your ability to build and work a process.

Remember: *a process that grows you as a person will grow you as a person.* Your odds for success increase. Your fulfillment in life can go up. Put in the time, the work and the focus on what you can control, and stop worrying about the results that you can't control.

You have to *practice*
small humility
to live out
big humility!

How to Get Along with Anyone

"Randy, I understand that officials will miss calls, yet the lack of professional, clear and respectful communication is unacceptable." As a Coordinator of Officials, I unfortunately hear this from coaches too often about officials. This is probably the most frustrating aspect and situation to deal with.

Surely, we are human and miss calls. We get it wrong; there I said it, we do make mistakes. Not all calls are great calls.

Sometimes we may not say the right thing. That is no excuse; however, for not remaining professional, clear and respectful. The coaches are right. It is unacceptable.

You want to know the greatest secret to becoming a successful official? It is the same secret in your line of work, and your life too.

Are you ready?

The very best ones that rise and stay at the top, the ones that become the leaders that others follow, the ones that never miss a great game all have one thing in common.

They know how to get along with anyone.

Anyone!

Like you, officials are professionals; therefore, we must be great, open, clear, and professional communicators. We need to move beyond our frustration to serve the cause. We have to be willing to look beyond the disagreement, and the personal opinions, and find common ground. We have to work well with others.

We have to focus on the relationship first, not just our expected results. We must care about people enough to want to get along with them.

In order to be fulfilled in your life, you need to know how to get along with anyone.

You do not live or work in a bubble by yourself. You interact, work with, live with and need to get along with others. You need to find collaboration, not conflict. You need to find resolution, not resistance. You need to build better relationships, not remain stuck, frustrated and bitter.

The challenge is, how do you do that with someone that disagrees with you?

How do you remain calm and professional when the other person is not?

How do you quickly respond to someone that is irrational and has biased emotion?

How do you, with so many differences, find the place of respect and resolution to move forward for the common goal?

How do you get along with anyone, anytime, anywhere?

We are really excited to share proven insights and techniques with you that will help you do just that. Before we get there, though, this next principle is paramount to your success in this area.

Let's be clear, what we are about to share will not work for any period of time or with any person if you don't take one foundational step:

Decide.

You need to decide that this is a top goal for you.

You need to decide that getting along with people is important in your daily life.

You need to decide, by setting your heart and your mind in the right place that others are important. They matter. Who they are and what they do is as important, if not more so, than yourself.

Decide that the goal is not winning the argument at all costs. The best thing for you to decide is that resolving situations for everyone's benefit is your goal.

You need to decide that getting along with everyone is the right way to live.

Here are three key strategies to improve your relationships and get along with anyone:

1. **You need to decide to be humble**

   Humility: freedom from excessive pride; the ability to serve others' interests as well as your own.

   There is no easy road to remaining humble. There is no easy button to considering the interests of others equal to or higher than yours.

   You must *decide* this is how you want to live and interact with others.

   In order to be humble in the big moments, you need to be humble in all of the little moments. You need to work it into your daily game, and practice your humble existence.

   It was March 2011, just before one of the last and biggest games for that season at the Division III level. As always, there were just the three of us making final preparations in the locker room. Three officials, who would soon head out to the court to be a part of an experience that only 9 officials enjoy once per year. The Final Four. It is an honor to be selected. It is also one of the highest pressure situations.

   It is truly very hard to describe.

   You know those rare moments when the world seems to be in slow motion? A time when your insides are excited, but a bit confused at the same time. A moment that you are so energized to begin, yet you almost don't want it to, because you know it will never happen again.

That was this moment.

Our crew chief that evening, Brian Kenney, put his arms around us. The three of us embraced, he prayed, and we walked into the arena.

The environment was electric. All of my family and several friends were in the crowd. It was such an honor to be there. The National anthem played, starting lineups were announced and then it was time to take the court for the work ahead.

Brian turns to me, hands me the ball, and says, "Randy, you go ahead and toss it."

I was stunned.

Tossing the ball to begin a Final Four game is a once in a lifetime moment. He knew how special it was. Again, I was stunned that he would give this up.

"Are you sure?" I asked.

His reply was a simple smile as he walked away.

I have a picture of the toss from that night. That one picture reminds of the game, the honor of being there, my career growth, the great work we did and, of course, that moment.

It also reminds me of kindness and humility. It may seem like a small gesture, yet it was a big act of humility. Brian made a decision to be humble. He thought of someone else (me) and my interests, not just his own.

Brian and I are still in contact with one another, and hardly is there a time that we speak when we don't relive that night. I still thank him for the opportunity and his humble leadership that day.

How do you live out humility?

Practice small ways to make a big difference for others through humility. Every day.

Picture this. You are heading to the check-out lane of the grocery store. You have 18 items and are in a hurry. You haven't allowed enough time for the fact the store only has one register open. The line is long. As you arrive, another shopper pulls up with her cart, overflowing with hundreds of items. She has three kids in tow, screaming, and the thought of being behind them curdles your stomach. The humble person allows the mom to go first, and does so with pleasure.

You have to practice small humility to live out big humility.

How about the roadway, when the semi truck driver turns on his signal and wants to slowly merge in front of you? You know they are traveling at least 20 miles an hour less than you, and it will take several minutes for them to pass the other slow driving semis. Regardless, you let him in. After he merges, he flashes his tail lights. The prideful and selfish person thinks,

"You better flash your lights and thank me, I let you in." The humble person thinks, "That was nice of him to thank me." In the end, by letting him in, that is the first small step toward setting your mind to humility. The hard part is also setting your heart. Your attitude and feeling about the action is what cements the act as one of true humility.

You wake up and start your day. You have many items on your agenda you want and need to accomplish. Someone very important in your life (spouse, friend, boss) has a different list of things for you to do. These things are important to them, and they need your help to accomplish them. Since this person is in your life, what matters to them must matter to you. The humble person will help with the list, and enjoy helping someone else accomplish their goals.

There is something amazing about being humble, since it is truly about not thinking highly of yourself. Remember this:

If you think you are humble, think again.

2. Apologies go a long way

Most people want to be right. They hold on to their beliefs and ideas because they want what they want.

Why? Because it can feel so good when we are right. So, we spend our time and energy proving and wanting to be right.

What would it feel like if you didn't try to prove or defend your position? What would it do for your ability to get along with others? What would happen if you were wrong?

The experience of making a mistake, of allowing another person to be right, or for you to end up being wrong is impactful. It changes relationships. It changes hearts. It changes everything, when done correctly.

"I am sorry."

"I was wrong."

Some of the greatest words that can be spoken to another human being.

When you truly apologize to someone it can be amazing how the interaction and relationship changes.

Check out this true story from a game Randy observed.

There were just 3 points separating the teams with minutes remaining. The visiting team had come back from 20 points down, and the energy and excitement was exhilarating. As the action went back and forth, from one end to the other, the coaches were now in the mode of closing out a victory. As usual, this typically involves stopping the action with a time out to make a game plan with the players.

With under a minute to go, the visiting team scores and requests a time out. The closest official runs past her, not granting the time out. The coach comes unglued. Thankfully, another official recognized her request and was able to grant the timeout.

Even though it was not that official's intent, by not hearing the coach, that official was unintentionally sending a message that they were no longer hearing or interested in what the coach had to say. Their lack of understanding and recognition of her needs put a strain on the relationship.

It is very hard to build a better relationship in these situations. This was a moment for those that want to get along with anyone to rise to the occasion; this official did just that.

Upon his partner blowing the whistle to award the timeout, he immediately walked over to the coach. Looking her in the eyes, with hands extended out and palms up, he simply and humbly said, "I apologize, coach, for not hearing you. I need to be better."

The coach's demeanor completely changed. She lowered her head and walked away. His ability to apologize, and be sincere in doing so, changed the attitude and perspective of the coach.

There is real power in an apology, when done *correctly*.

Simple steps to a successful apology:

- Look the person in the eye
- Calm your voice and use approachable body language
- Ask, "Will you accept my apology?"
- Resolve to take steps moving forward that will prevent the mistake from repeating

No excuses. No blame. Nothing, except ownership, remorse, and a resolve to do and be better.

Let's flip the coin.

You also need to be able to forgive others. No matter what is done, or said, or how poor another person's apology is, forgive them.

You don't need to forget, but you can forgive.

If we expect people to forgive us, we must first start by being willing to forgive others.

People make mistakes. They say and do stupid things. They can, and maybe rightly so, tick us off. People let us down. Oh, we can make a long list.

If you want to get along with anyone, if you want freedom in your relationships, freedom to move forward and have success, you need to forgive.

A good apology and a willingness to forgive are a powerful combination to reducing conflict, increasing trust, decreasing emotions and ultimately improving relationships.

The choice is up to you. You can decide to forgive, you can decide to apologize, or not. The decision is yours.

3. **Climbing to a better relationship involves a LADR**

It is commonplace in basketball games for there to be disagreement, questioning and outright complaining from coaches towards officials.

The reality is that the referees have control of what is or isn't called. That lack of control can cause frustration from a coach. They are so passionate and emotionally invested in their players, the game and their goals, they can sometimes lose sight of officials being human beings.

You likely have similar situations in your life. Someone disagrees with you or vice versa. Even though you are both experiencing or observing the exact same situation, you have completely different perspectives than others in your life. Arguments can ensue, and become personal because of the strong positions you have. Then you add stressed, overworked, tired, and fallible human beings, and you have a formula for a volcanic explosion.

As we have stated before, there is a decision you must make. A set of choices that help you climb into a better relationship, or fall deeper into a dark place.

You have choices to fight for victory, or to fight for resolution; to argue and prove a point, or to discuss to better understand; to make your case be known, or to hear another perspective.

Choices. Decisions. To climb or to fall.

The referees that are considered some of the best in the business are the best at handling these moments. They defuse most situations better than others, because they know how to climb.

Climbing a ladder involves steps. One step at a time.

Improving relationships to get along with anyone is similar. It is one step at a time. Rising higher and higher as you continue the climb.

This climb; however, isn't about a ladder of success. It is a metaphorical ladder of the core techniques required to get along with anyone in the most difficult moments.

The ladder (LADR) is the acronym of four specific and proven steps to help you on your journey.

Before we unveil the details, recognize that you do have alternate methods. These are long and commonly used, *failed* methods that somehow continue to resurface despite their poor record. Check out this non-fiction interaction.

"Jeff, that is a foul! Why didn't you call that?" exclaimed the coach.

Jeff keeps sprinting down the floor, not looking back or pausing. He does nothing and says nothing. He tries to pretend he didn't hear her. He hides. He ignores.

This is option one that many people take in life.

Ignore.

They simply ignore the other person. There is no response. Zero acknowledgment.

Question for you. *Do you love being ignored?*

Dumb question, right? Of course not! You want to be heard. You want to know that you exist for a purpose and that your life has value.

So does everyone else.

Here's a genius idea, let's remove *ignoring* from our list of strategies!

Another popular, yet failed concept, is the person that always wants to win. They just have to be right. No matter what is said, their idea, their statement, their opinion and their expectation is all that matters.

If we're honest, we all have a difficult time with these people. They are never wrong, quick to blame, fight to win, and are rarely concerned with the team.

Let's take another look at our coach and official interaction.

"Jeff, that is a foul! Why didn't you call that?"

Without even letting the coach finish, Jeff is already exclaiming and defending, "No it isn't, coach. That isn't a foul."

Now with increased animation and volume the coach is more heated and yells, "Jeff, I saw *and heard* my player get hit!"

"No, coach, I saw it, she did *not* get hit."

"Yes she did, oh my, you are terrible!"

"That's enough coach, we're done!!!"

You can see this conversation is going nowhere; other than a technical foul. This is not an exchange or a conversation. This is simply standing on point to win.

When it comes to relationships, there is not a winner when we only try to win.

Don't be one of those people.

Winning *isn't* the goal.

The process that has been proven to build relationships for ongoing success is called LADR:

L = Listen

A = Acknowledge

D = Discuss

R = Resolve

You need to *listen* to others.

You need to *acknowledge* their position.

You need to *discuss* as much as possible.

Most importantly, head these words:

Your goal is to *resolve* the situation in a manner that builds the relationship up as best you can.

Resolve, not ignore. Resolve, not fight. Resolve, not win.

Listen. When we listen, we must truly listen.

1. Make eye contact, and stop moving if you can

2. Ensure your body language is open, with eyebrows raised, palms up, arms unfolded, never crossed

3. Hear everything the other person says, and everything they don't say, listen for what they mean

4. Stop thinking about what you want to say, listen fully and then respond

Acknowledge.

1. Say things to let them know they are being heard, such as: ok, I hear you, tell me more, I understand, that is a valid point, fair enough

2. Make movements that affirm you are listening and hear them: nod your head up and down, smile, lean slightly toward them, show compassion

3. Give them credit for a good idea, or a perspective you don't have that could be a good one to consider

Discuss.

1. Ask them questions

2. Respond to their answers with your true thoughts, in a positive manner to generate more discussion

3. Be open to their perspective

4. Ask them more questions

5. Listen and acknowledge (you see how the cycle repeats)

Resolve. Resolutions look different in every situation, yet your goal is for both parties to feel ok with the outcome. The winning versus losing game is not one to be played.

Instead, stay focused on resolving by:

1. Finding common ground

2. Agreeing to disagree where it doesn't hurt the vision and future plans

3. Seeking and focusing on mutual goals and how you can help one another reach them

4. Hearing and appreciating their interests and what their perspectives are

Let's utilize LADR with our made up official coach interaction.

"Jeff, that is a foul! Why didn't you call that?"

Jeff responds with, "What did I miss?"

Notice that Jeff offers a question showing openness rather than be defensive. He didn't say, "What did you see that I missed?" He just says, "What did I miss?" Additionally, by asking a question, and then truly listening for the answer he is prepared for the next step in LADR.

With a raised voice and arm gestures to provide a visual, the coach exclaims, "She reached down and hit my player on the arm; I heard it and saw it."

With an expression of empathy and truthful frustration, Jeff replies with, "Oh my gosh, if that happened, I missed it. I do NOT want to miss plays like that."

The coach comes back with, "This game is too important for that, you have to get those, Jeff."

"I couldn't agree more, I need to be stronger in that area."

Maybe the player was hit, maybe not. The film will tell, but in the moment, this isn't an argument to win.

Look back at this interaction again. Never once did Jeff say, "no, I didn't", or "you are wrong, coach," or anything to further excite, ignore or fuel the conversation for a personal win. Everything he did was to show compassion and empathy, by listening, acknowledging, discussing and resolving. Jeff uses LADR in the moment to resolve the situation so the relationship can be improved and rapport is maintained.

Trust and respect are built when you listen.

Value and worth are affirmed when you acknowledge.

A relationship forms and grows out of honest discussion.

Resolutions for the long run build relationships.

LADR will help you get along with anyone.

You can learn from this. You can use these techniques to be better in small and big moments in your life.

Saying that; however, what do you do when people still choose to be rude, disrespectful, and inconsiderate?

What do you do when you work the processes we have outlined, and nothing seems to change?

How do you continue to build into others with tenants of humility, apology and the LADR system when they *still* don't, or won't, change?

What do you do when someone believes it is all about them?

How do you get along with *that* kind of person?

You read the next chapter.

Caring about someone means caring about *who they are,* not about *what they do.*

Love, I Didn't See it Coming

You love them anyway.

"I love you."

The three greatest words you can speak to a human being.

Saying 'I love you' tends to be a phrase which is saved for the love of our lives. It is said by parents to children (and vice versa) as well as other members of our family. We find it written in the note the teacher intercepts between two 2nd graders. Typically, the words are reserved for the special moments and only the very special people in our lives.

Rarely, do we hear people share this sentiment with co-workers, friends, neighbors and those not as close to their personal lives. Love is not a word we find in most company vision statements or business plans. It isn't something we commonly express to people we see infrequently. Surely, *I love you* is not something we easily toss-out to those outside our inner circle.

It is strange that in a world and society with so much hurt and divide, the emotion of loving someone or something publicly seems to have been restricted, almost like an embarrassment. The word itself seems to have been reduced to like, enjoy or some other word that doesn't contain nearly as much feeling from the heart.

So, in light of this seemingly unlovable world, we ask this:

What do you love to do?

Who do you love?

What makes life worth the love of living?

As you ponder those thoughts, we would love to share with you how love, and sharing it from the heart, has changed our lives and the lives of those around us.

After reading this book, it should not come as a surprise how much Jeff and I love the game of basketball.

For me, this "love of the game" came at a very young age. I remember watching my favorite players on TV as a boy. From the DePaul Blue Demons to the Chicago Bulls, I loved to watch the game.

When I was in grade school my father was the assistant coach. I couldn't get enough of the game and the atmosphere in the gym. I loved sitting behind the bench at Wheaton North High School as the team manager. I thought I was among celebrities with the high school players. Part of the mystique was that one day, I would be at that same high school. I would play in that gym. I would wear that uniform.

Truth be told, I was on the team, but spent more time grabbing pine splinters than rebounds.

As a freshman in college, my friend that lived next door to me was a huge sports nut. We talked about Michael Jordan and the Bulls winning ways, dreaming about how many championships could be in their future. This was the late 80's, so we were somewhat prophetic of what was to come, or at least we thought.

From this connection, and the need for extra money in college, he and I started officiating basketball games in town at the local schools. That began a whole other love for the game. Like Jeff Cross, I was hooked. I couldn't get enough. I quickly moved into higher level games, learned from failure and did everything I could to be the best communicator possible.

Looking back, I have been so blessed. In my career, I've worked over 1,000 games, including an appearance at the NCAA Division II Regionals, and becoming the Coordinator of Officials for multiple Division III conferences. Now, to be clear, it was not all rainbows and unicorns. I failed, many times. I had hard days, and still do. I had long weeks thinking about the big call I kicked or the rule that was incorrectly adjudicated. By all means, I didn't get to where I am alone.

You want to know what got me through?

Love.

Love of the game. Love from family and friends. Knowing I am loved by God for who I am and not for what I did or didn't do.

Love.

That friend from college, his name is Jeff Mikyska, we've been friends ever since. He is a pastor and actually led the service to marry my wife and I all those years ago. We don't always see each other as often as we used to; sometimes a year or two passes. We recently had dinner at his home, and it was like we hadn't missed a moment, we just picked right back up.

I'm sure you have some friends like that yourself. People who you pick up with where you left off and thoroughly enjoy, no matter what happens or how long it's been. People you love and respect.

I know that love of the game is not the same as love for people, yet I do love the game. I love the journey and memories it has provided. I love the action of a close game and working hard to be in position to make the right call in the right moment.

With all that said, when I put away the whistle, the game will go on. Someone else will work those games. It will be time for someone else to receive the opportunities and the fun. Time for the next generation to ensure they don't miss a great game.

I might miss some of the action, but probably not the pressure of night after night decisions.

I promise you this, though, I know I will miss the one thing the game has provided to me the most.

Friendships.

I will miss the people. The love I have for each of them; for who they are, and how they make the experiences unique, fun and memorable. I will miss those long rides, the longer phone calls, the laughter, the tears, and the high fives.

You know, spending two hours getting yelled at while trying to perform at a high level is hard work. Working hard with other people to serve a highly competitive game is hard work. To make this hard work even more challenging, we have different partners for nearly every game. Many times, our partners could be complete strangers, other times, friends we have known for years.

Being an official creates a unique bond, the experience of being in a family that we share.

Here is why this truth of love for these people is so real for me.

The differences in our political views, our education background, our culture, the color of our skin, our age, our economic status, you name it; they don't matter. In a world that can be divisive, and focuses on blame and pointing out differences, there is something wonderful that happens in a locker room before a game.

From getting dressed in that common uniform of black and white stripes, with black shoes, a black whistle and black pants, we seem to be identical. Yet, we know, we are 3 unique people bringing our life experiences to work. We need to (and do) find a way to be effective together.

That continues with bonds of trust and respect on the court. Trusting that we will take care of our portion of the work. Trusting judgment not to believe one of us is right or better. Trusting that the game is better served as a team.

Bottom line, it's not about us. The best officials know they are there to serve. Just love the game and the people, that's it.

And then these relationships just grow after the games, in conversations, at summer camps and throughout a career. The love keeps growing when you CARE enough about the people.

Just like you. You work, and live life, with people that may be very different than you. You show up to contribute, to do your best work, in order to make a difference. You want life to go well, to do good and to be given respect as you give it.

We are the same.

Officials are a team.

As such, we all need to find common ground, respect and trust in order to be successful. In order for there to be love.

That starts with an intentional focus, a proper perspective, and discipline to manage your thoughts, your actions and your words. It takes practice. It takes a heart to care enough about the work and the people more than yourself.

As you develop and continue relationships, both short and long-term, both in your professional and personal life, this acronym will help you strengthen those bonds.

C.A.R.E.

You need to C.A.R.E.

Which stands for **Create Authentic Relationships** with **Everyone**.

This isn't the, "Hey, how ya' doin'?" interaction. This is a genuine care for someone; concern for how they feel, and what they desire. A care for their worth as a person and for the value they bring.

We'd like to share a true story from Jeff's life that helps illustrate this kind of love.

I remember meeting my baseball partner when I was still a teenager. I frequented the local fields as often as I could. I loved watching the games and watching the umpires. Not only was it fun, it also helped me improve.

One Saturday, while I was standing in my usual spot along the fence, one of the umpires came to the fence to discuss the situation regarding a play.

I remember listening to him explain why he ruled the way he did in that specific situation and being amazed how he explained it to the coach and others involved. I thought to myself, "That is what I want to be like: calm, controlled and confident."

I wanted to be out on the field and have such confidence when talking to others and have such knowledge for the rules that no one would doubt me. Furthermore, they would respect me, not because I wanted the status, but because I earned the respect for the work I had put in preparing to serve the game, the job and the people.

Later that summer, this same guy pulled into the garage where I worked to get some gas for his car. I was working behind the counter, watching him while he pumped his gas. I just knew I had to meet him.

I mustered up the courage, ran outside and went right up to him and said, "Aren't you Sam?"

With a bit of hesitation, pulling away from me, as he had no idea who this strange kid was approaching him, he confirmed he was indeed Sam.

With great excitement, I continued to dive into this new relationship. See, I knew Sam had been to professional umpire school and I just couldn't wait for him to be my friend.

I nearly shouted at him, exclaiming, "My name is Jeff, and I am going to go to professional umpire school!"

Having no idea who I was at the time, and, if I'm being honest, I'm not sure Sam cared. He didn't say much. Through this dramatic pause, he was probably thinking that I was some sort of wacko, and he was just struggling to even figure out what was the purpose of this meeting.

I have to say, the meeting didn't go as I had imagined in my mind. I walked away wondering if Sam even spoke. Yet, it opened a door.

As we fast forward over 30 years later Sam and I are great friends. He is close to a decade older than me, and has taught me, helped me and simply been there for me through so much of life.

We have worked hundreds of games together, both baseball and basketball. We have spent countless hours on the phone talking about all sorts of things; so much so, that our wives compare us to a couple of teenage girls.

Here is the main point about Sam.

He didn't need to be my friend. He had already made his run.

He didn't need a little snot-nosed teenager tugging after him. He could have ignored me. Or, he even could have used me for connections, for status, for his pride, or even to make it appear that he was helping build up the next generation.

No, not Sam.

See, he cared about me. He cared about my family, my health, my future. He cared about the person, Jeff Cross.

Caring about someone means caring about who they are, not about what they do.

Now it's Randy's turn to share...

It was the fall of 2006, and I had recently lost my first wife, Dawne, to cancer. We had been together for nearly 20 years. She was just 36 years old.

Yet, it was a lifetime for her. And what a life she had.

She cared for so many.

While fighting this fight, with month after month of chemo that took just about every ounce of strength, she never complained. As her body began to fade, she still carried herself with dignity and grace. To the end, she was concerned for how everyone would carry on, not at all worried about her own death.

That's love.

The last few months had been very, very difficult. Watching someone you love decline until death is one of life's toughest tasks. And I didn't always handle things well. I could have said more, been more patient, more understanding…loved a bit more.

Sometimes, when we are pushed by really hard things, we don't always take the best step forward. Again, from failure, we can learn *and do* better next time.

Both her family and mine, the extended Fox family, were wonderful. They showed up and helped out a great deal. They did everything they could to care for her, lift me up, make the boys (who were very young) feel that life could still have hope.

I am grateful for each and every one of them, and all of our friends, who loved us. Mostly, I'm thankful for how God moved. He changed me. He brought a new awareness of life, of love and purpose.

Who meant more than what. *Why* meant more than how. Perspective came in, priorities were brought in order, and life had a different vantage point for me than it did before.

The days sped along after she passed. Fall came quickly and the basketball season was fast approaching.

I clearly remember being asked by a family member, "Are you going to officiate this year?"

I replied "I don't officiate basketball, I *am* a basketball official."

For me, the game had been a part of my entire life. Officiating wasn't just something I did, it was part of me; a huge part of the previous 20 years. At that critical time, I simply needed my officiating family, and the love for the game.

A couple of weeks later, as I walked into Lake Forest College for the preseason central region officiating meeting, I saw over 100 friends. Faces I hadn't seen in months, maybe years. Everyone gathered in this place to prepare for another year, with excitement and anticipation.

Many of them came up to me at some point that day. With hugs, some tears and a tremendous amount of support.

I knew I had made the right decision.

The love shared that day was so needed; it boosted my spirits, and provided fuel to move forward.

Yet I had no idea that God had bigger plans for me that season than just loving the game and feeling better for a day.

The meeting was starting, and it was time to find a seat. I climbed to the top of the bleachers, worked my way in the crowd and sat down by some officials I actually didn't know well, or at all.

Marne Boario, from Madison Wisconsin, was seated directly to my left. We talked on and off during the meeting. We had worked a game together some time back, yet we hadn't seen each other in several years. We connected that day in a way that was uplifting.

As we were leaving Marne mentioned, "I'm coming to Illinois to work some games in a month or so, maybe we could meet up somewhere for dinner?"

"Sure, sounds fun, reach out to me," was my reply back.

A few days later, an email popped up in my inbox from Marne. She was following back up with the dates she would be in my area and wanted to see if anything fit with my schedule.

I began typing my reply. About five lines in, something moved me. Before I knew it, I was searching the officiating database for her number, my hand was on my cell phone and the phone was ringing.

To my surprise, she picked up. She had no idea who was calling, but she answered.

We talked for about an hour, which became known as a rather short conversation for us. We agreed on a date about a month out that we would meet for dinner.

The following Sunday evening, I had just put my boys to bed and was finally sitting down to watch a little TV. Suddenly, my phone rang. It was a number I didn't recognize.

For some crazy reason, I picked up.

It was Marne.

About 10 minutes into the call, I realized this conversation, and the planned dinner, had more interest for her than just a convenient way to see another referee.

She was interested! In me!

To be honest, I actually started to get nervous. I paced the floor in my kitchen like a caged lion waiting for feeding time. I began to shake!

Thirty-seven years old and I'm anxious talking to a girl like I was just twelve.

The good news is that the conversation flowed from one topic to the next. We laughed and laughed some more. A little over three hours later we decided that rest would do us some good.

I went to work the next day, and all I could think about was her. I tried to go on a date with someone else, absolute disaster! I tried to talk to someone else; felt like I was listening to a clucking hen. All I could do was think of Marne.

It was crazy.

I thought I needed some time, some room to breathe, that sounded like it would be good after everything that happened. Again, God had other plans. Sometimes in life, we need to throw our plans for the future out the window and just care for those in our lives at that moment.

This was not the plan. Like Jeanna did to Jeff, I tried to resist.

To no avail.

Even though we hadn't been on one date in person, Marne had captured my heart.

I called Marne a couple nights later. We talked again for hours, and during that call, I secretly managed to move my schedule around. I surprised Marne a couple days later with news that I was coming up to Madison, the next day, for our first official date.

It was amazing.

Life-changing.

Unexpected.

A blessing.

Fast forward seven months of dating, hours of phone calls and sharing, and our love for one another grew strong. I couldn't do enough for her. We were married that spring.

In no way did I see this coming. In no way did I expect to fall in love again, and so quickly, and to be blessed with another amazing woman.

Marne adopted both of the boys, Trevor and Brendon, so we could be a family unit.

Love from her to us.

Five years later, we were blessed with a little girl and just knew that was God's way of solidifying our family even further with His love. We named her Nevaeh.

Now, 11 years later, I can just pinch myself over this journey. I cannot think of my life much better than it is.

Oh, and love, yeah, lots of love. All the glory to God for providing, and nearly provoking me, to say yes to her invitation.

Marne and I had the game of basketball in common, and we connected at a time I least expected it. It proves that when any of us are open to new possibilities, when we trust people, when we enjoy the moments and don't miss the great game; we get even more than we hoped or imagined.

The game of basketball in the season of 2006 – 2007 brought me a new life, a new wife, and a new love.

Not sure I can express enough about my love for Marne and the life we have together. I am forever thankful for her.

I know Jeff agrees with me, when all is said and done, the greatest game we don't want to miss is *the game of life*. The once in a lifetime journey that provides such joy, when we give love first. We hope you agree with us:

The life you get is the life you give. Love comes to those that love.

The bottom line: you need, we need, the world needs *more* love.

Why?

We don't want to miss a great game.

You want to maximize your work, your life, your relationships?

In the end, success in life comes down to love.

Do you love yourself?

Do you love what you do?

Do you love others?

Our definition of success:

Love the life you live, and love those you live it with.

Enjoy the journey, each and every moment. Remember that failure is an option, success takes time, leaders build the tower for success, the inner game is what fuels the outer game, and the key points of LADR for getting along with anyone.

With all that, never forget this most important truth: *in the end, it all comes down to love.*

Never miss a great game.

Never!

To us, basketball has meant so much. The wonderful games, the rising journey, and most importantly, the friendships.

We are so thankful you have joined us, as we've unpacked life lessons on and off the court.

As you enjoy your game of life, remember the world is waiting for you…to love.

Love
the *life* you *live*
and *love* those
you live it *with*.

Epilogue

Walking through the open door to write this book was a huge step for me (Jeff), and co-authoring a project was totally new for Randy.

I thought for nearly 10 years about writing a book, but I was scared. So many unknowns, so many thoughts about what people would think of my work. Would they even like it?

After Randy's call to work together, I realized this was something I wanted to do and fear was holding me back. I wanted this, so I needed to do this.

When we have a passion for people and something in life, it is amazing how we find people around us that want to help.

If we will let them.

We are so thankful for all of you who decided to take this journey with us. Have you now thought more about your journey?

You have things you are still thinking about doing. Here is what we know to be true:

Once we decided to take this on, the biggest step we did is the same thing you must do to enjoy the great game of life.

Start.

Simply begin.

Take one step, even if it is small.

It is amazing how experiences become far less monumental than we think when we just put one foot in front of the other.

As you step forward in life and face the games before you, never forget that missing the great game starts by not showing up. We finish with the same powerful quote with which we began:

Enjoying the great game of life means we show up. We play. We are open to discovering the learnings and principles that will help us along the way. We learn, we keep going, and we fall in love with life.

Not missing a great game can be hard. No, it is hard. It takes intentional work on the processes and methodologies we have covered.

The hard work, though, produces results.

So, for the sake of your great game of life, please show up! Stay the course and whatever you do, keep going. Simply put...

Do hard things.

Randy and Jeff
May 2018

Acknowledgments

I am thankful to my wife, Marne, and my three children, Trevor, Brendon and Nevaeh, for how you all make life worth living. I love what I do, yet I love you all more. Here is to our next adventure doing the work God gives us to do!

This is truly one of my favorite books to date. What fun, what joy it has been to work with you, Jeff Cross, on this project. Your wisdom is such a blessing. Thank you, my friend, for being a great part of my life; oh yeah, and for doing this with me!

Aurelie, you just get me! Always thankful for your talent, your insight, and your spirit. This project has the *Irish Eyes Design* touch and I am blessed for that. Thank you for believing in and supporting me.

Calvary, you have lifted so many weights off my back, allowing time for me to do what I do best. Appreciate you, your heart and all your investment as Business Manager, Marketing Manager, and more. Everything you do gets rave reviews from clients, and I am thankful you're a key part of the team!

Thank you, the reader, for reading this. A bigger thank YOU as you take these lessons and use them in your life. Together, we make a difference, each and every day.

-Randy

There have been several friends and family that have shown up to encourage me throughout my life, on and off the court. In fact, that would be a long list.

While I would like to thank those on that list and let them know they are appreciated, I also need to send a special shout-out to Sam Nicholos, Corky Schreiner and Abby Burmeister; thank you for being there, for always answering my phone calls, for being ready to listen and support me in my decisions. While some would see an unreachable goal, you would make me feel like I was unstoppable and you continue to challenge me to reach the next level.

Thanks to Randy Fox for making this specific goal come to fruition.

Thanks to my wife, Jeanna, for showing up, sticking around, and supporting me through this journey. I am grateful we get to experience this game of life together!

Jeff Cross brings a broad perspective to life through his career in intercollegiate and interscholastic sports. He is in his fifteenth year as a Division I NCAA Women's Basketball official, is the Athletic Director at a private school, and coached multiple high school sports.

These experiences, and a love for both the game and the participants, have led him to many leadership and teaching roles with adults and students.

Beyond coaching and officiating, Jeff uses his people-skills to teach at camps and schools for officials, speak to audiences on communication, teamwork and overcoming failure, and help people be successful in life.

He has been afforded the honor to work 25+ NCAA post-season games, a WNIT Elite Eight, and the NCAA Division I National Tournament.

Jeff, his wife Jeanna, and their two adult children are loving the game of life!

As a professional speaker and author Randy Fox uses his leadership experience and energy to engage audiences and transform their leadership.

With a twenty-year career as a corporate leader and NCAA basketball official, Randy has a wealth of knowledge and a unique perspective on effective leadership. His focus is team building and advocating for the potential in all workers in order to turn everyday people into superstar leaders.

Randy is a professional member of the National Speakers Association, and the author of several noteworthy leadership books, including *Game Plan, A Leader Worth Following, Refined by Fire,* and *Soul On Fire.* To schedule Randy for a speaking engagement or learn more about other resources, go to:

www.foxpoint.net

Enjoying the great game
of life
means we show up.
We *play*. We are *open*
to discovering the
learnings and principles
that will help us along the way.
We *learn,*
we keep going and we fall
in love with life.